WHIRLWIND

For Julie —
may your poetry
blossom
happily, not at
the Pudge.

11 Oct. '12

PITT POETRY SERIES

Ed Ochester, Editor

WHIRLWIND

SHARON DOLIN

UNIVERSITY OF PITTSBURGH PRESS

Published by the University of Pittsburgh Press, Pittsburgh, Pa., 15260
Copyright © 2012, Sharon Dolin
All rights reserved
Manufactured in the United States of America
Printed on acid-free paper
10 9 8 7 6 5 4 3 2 1

ISBN 13: 978-0-8229-6221-2
ISBN 10: 0-8229-6221-7

In memory of my father, Irving Dolin (1923–2011)

"You pick, and you pick, and you pick . . . and you fall in."

Can you know anything that is not deception?
Once deception was destroyed, you wouldn't
be able to look, at the risk of turning into a
pillar of salt.

–Franz Kafka, The Zürau Aphorisms

Contents

III. Happiness Is Luck

WHIRLWIND

I. Smudging

Ode to Nitrous Oxide

Coleridge said that nitrous oxide—laughing gas—
provided "the most unmingled pleasure" he ever knew.

Is it only the memory of being
ten and being driven to Manhattan
to see the "dintist," as the elevator man
called him—the one time I can recall being
in a building with an elevator—that invokes you?
Or is it the pain I feared then or the pain I flee from now—
tooth pain, the whirring drill, or the agonizing ache of hearing
my husband just having had a housewarming party with another
woman in another apartment—the one I don't have the keys to?
Is it about laughing over the pain or about *Gonna take you higher,*
as Sly said in the Sixties when I thought I was too young to smoke
yet there I was snorting that sweet stuff up in the dentist's chair
on what must have been the Upper East Side—this Brooklyn girl
from East Flatbush—and loving it. It felt like soft rubber wrapping
around my face around as the dentist drilled around & around drilled
& wiggled his nose & whiskers like a human bunny rabbit.
                                        Here I am now,
forty years later, asking for it in another East Side building where my name
is announced. Asking to be put out of my pain—to feel the numbness flower
down my arms into my pelvis. Isn't it funny how good numb can feel? Is *that*
the experience? Or is it waking up after—lucid but no longer asking (or caring)
where it throbs—or when—or why—or because of whom.

To the Furies Who Visited Me in the Basement of Duane Reade

I bow and give thanks—not as moth to the flame
but as the singeing flame   You made me quake as I stood
        with my dog waiting behind the line to get to the counter.   Stuck

as if struck with palsy between the painkillers and
the glasses for close reading   I spied there   waiting at the Drop-Off
        line—or was it the Pick-Up line—the two of them   fluttering eyes

at each other in their blind love-bubble: she—whom I had never
seen before   now   in profile   with her serpentine
        graying hair gazing up at him   who had   twelve years

before   almost to the day   gazed in and given me a ring   and who still
wore the ring I had given him   *I am my Beloved's*
        inscribed within.   Now which Beloved was *that?*

O Eumenides, You swelled my head and heart with seething African bees.
(inside Apollo whispered, "You can just leave, walk back
        upstairs.")   But You steaming, stunned me: voices

of Medea, of Clytemnestra, of Dido, of Circe, of Judith,
of Tamar, of Ariadne, of Electra, of Agave You all buzzed
        all clamored as I watched them

for the longest five minutes of my life: as intimate
as the yolk and white inside an uncracked egg—they could
        have been in bed

until   after a century   he turned from the counter
to encounter my gaze and without a flicker of . . .
        with no nod to me who was still his wife—as though he foresaw

what was coming—as unavoidable and elastic as seconds before a crash—
as though he could shield her from the blowtorch of our collective rage
        took her shoulder—the as-yet blind, limping one

the weak woman as I had once been (before You possessed me)—the one
who had not seen me—who had never seen me—to guide her
        down another aisle:

YOU FUCKING BITCH!   with death-heat blast   shrieked out
Alecto   Tisiphone   Megaera
        so she had to turn—look up at me   look

at all the women betrayed by other women—
at first blank-faced as though blindsided by a stranger
        then a shutter of recognition so she veered

away as though I were radioactive   rabid
and might bite her.   I bow and give thanks to You,
        O Dirae   for giving me daggermouth

and the scornful heart that no longer cares
what he thinks of me when I cared for too long.
        And I let Your fury seizure through me

like the first pain-shiver of labor   or some earth-tremor.
Abandoned wife but not unsexed.
        Come, You winged goddesses in Your short kid skirts

and huntress boots: Re-sex me here—not suppliant—
with my one-headed dog ready to take down
    to Hell any man or woman who dares deceive and kill

my love. Let me rise into the moonlight—shake frenzied breasts   arms
ass   in a belly dance with Your Maenads and piping goatmen.

The Tip

That he left it behind when he left.
That it has three teeth.
That it might be the horny snout-end of a defunct dragon.
That I remember him, early on, putting it in and turning it when it broke off.
That he looked at me and said, *Uh-oh. She doesn't want us to get in.*
That he went downstairs and had a new one made.
That he saved the body and the tip in a reliquary bowl beside her photo and urn.
That it slept beside his old wedding band.
Even after I had moved in.
That it lived on an altar with us for thirteen years.
That he took its body with him.
That anything can become a relic.
That I never understood until now he must have been afraid of her ghost.
That our son found it on the hall table the other night and said, *Uh-oh.*
That I said, *It's okay. Just leave it there.*
That I am writing these lines as a way to deconsecrate it.
To bury it by revealing it.
That when I have finished I am throwing it in the trash.
That his laptop became the new Ark containing the new Holy of Holies.
That around the Ides of March he installed a code, he said, to keep his son out.
That I knew it was to keep me out.
That he got angry when I called to have lunch with him.
That the tip of him was already gone.
That he was giving it to her after lunch.
That he threw me off the scent in an e-mail saying, *I'll never sleep with her. I'll never
    replace you with her.*
That his words were a purloined letter.
That I still believe in the gold standard for language.

That he counted on that.
That the dead beating heart was his.
That he refused to read my lines.
That I've changed the top dead-bolt.
That he now has a new one he puts inside a new lock in a new door.
That she has one too.
That I still haven't changed the bottom lock.
That it would still fit in.
That it would get lost. Might jam it, with no body to turn it.
That I won't test it out.
That it holds my smelted rage.
That it all comes down to a minuscule piece of brass.

After My Husband Moved Out His Things

my son dropped
       the tiny sponge Buddha inside
the largest Mason jar we had
       after filling it to the brim with
water then locked down the lid.

Each day the Buddha—a sitting frog
       battening on water—
grew inside his tank
       as I'm sure the boy wished
his father would grow inside his heart,

our house—a talisman to lure him
       back. We never spoke of it.
He never wanted to speak of any of it.
       After a week he emptied out the jar
set the distended Buddha—size of a rubber

ducky, color of runoff foam on a
       clear pond—on the sink's edge
and forgot about it
       as the air slowly
shriveled the figure:

first the head—as the water
       weighed down its sodden robes—
until it was the size of a desiccated
       thumb—hard as a stale eraser.

Unpairing: Proofreading My Marriage

Change *paired* to ... *despaired.*
Cleaved to ... *cleaved apart.*
Seen to ... *ob/scene.*
Trust to ... *rust.*
Change *Honor* to ... *Your Honor.*
Lover to ... *voleur.*
Mattress to ... *Maîtresse.*
Under his thumb to ... *Sunder him, numb.*
Martyr to ... *Mar her.*
Husband to ... *"Us" banned.*
Weaver to ... *deceiver.*
We aver to ... *We abhor.*
Change *Forever* to ... *For never.*
For better or worse to ... *Far better, divorce.*
Change *eternal bond* to ... *infernal fond.*
Change *Adults are us* to ... *Adulterous.*
Change *domestic bliss* to ... *Oh what a mess is this!*
What's mine is yours to ... *What's yours is mine.*
Change *dependable* to ... *expendable.*
Change *loyal* to ... *lawyer.*
Change *nuclear family* to ... *Nuke our family.*
Terra firma to ... *Error, former.*
Change *ketuba* to ... *Get a get.*
Domesticity to ... *duplicity.*
Change *fourth wife* to ... *Forfeit wife.*
Change *his analyst* to ... *his anal tryst.*
Change *her pissed* to ... *herpes.*
Change *dirty laundry* to ... *tawdry.*

His ethics to . . . *his antics.*
Her ethics to . . . *heretics.*
Love poems to . . . *woe zone.*
Change *woe zone* to . . . *war zone.*
Till death do us part to . . . *Come Death, do your art!*

First Words, Last Words

Do you think you can teach me with words?
Is a speech of despair just wind?
>   —The Book of Job

Why do you expect people to behave well? The first words
he ever said to me after a man, a famous New Age man,
had raged at me: had heaved a crystal vase with two hands—
like Moses heaving the first tablets of the law—down
into my knapsack on the floor. *Here! Take* this *as collateral!*
After I had asked for an i.o.u. for the work I had done. *This*

the story I was telling at dinner after the art opening
of canvases resembling corroded doors scored
by love's wars. This the first time I met my then-future husband,
now my soon-to-be ex-husband. There the two of us sat:
he, happily married, I, just engaged. How we gazed at each other
and thought, *That's my kind of. . . if only I were free.*

In a month my fiancé crashed his heart with coke.
In a year his wife turned to ash when her plane crashed.
If I were writing this as a novel would you believe it?
Or would you back away at the tragic coincidence?
I am here to tell you it happened; it does happen.
It happened to me. Which is not why I can make anything of it.

But don't we always want to make something of the wounds in our lives?
I already have those words elsewhere, the words he said,
Why do you expect someone to treat you well?
Said like he was a Buddhist Sphinx—or was it just foresight
or self-knowledge or self-deceit. I am a reader. How can I not be
haunted by those words fourteen years later. How like

the harsh wind of him blowing through the ribcage
I tried to embrace even after he'd left. Which is the worst thing
he said to me at the end: *I've lost all empathy for you*? Or, when
I asked him to give us a week—to give his wife, his son, his marriage
one week in Wellfleet as we walked out on that windblown shore—
not to speak to his mistress for one week: *I can't do that.* She's

in too much pain? Or does it remain his first question transmuted—the words
of the whirlwind—hanging desiccated in the mist all fall,
the bitterest fruit I have ever tasted:
                    Why did I expect my husband
to treat me well? Isn't that why I heaved all night in a pail
after I dragged it out of him, that he was fucking her in Athens (no way
to pretty this up), while I stayed behind with our son on Naxos, the island

of Bacchic rites? To which he responded, as out of the heart's void—
(and I wish I were making it up): *Maybe you have food poisoning.*

Scenes from an Ideal Marriage

after Cy Twombly, 1986

I. Ideal

Ideal because it's hard to tell
    what's there. On Wherever Lane
        we read a reader in with a
sofa or reclining chair—back
    to the ringing chaos that's
        the smudgy forest of home life.
Gender is obsolete. And the child
    rules the living room.
        It's always possible to make French
toast. Maple syrup drips like paint
    over our days—and white nights?
        We've had so many they color
our view—rouged with naps,
    stippled with flowers. Watch your
        back: The child-prince is about
to wield a bat.

II. Anything Goes

> out the window (except the child)
> the order of newspaper sections the
mail arriving by 3, your after-dinner
> drink or lozenge of chocolate.
> Jump rope of plastic cups the fetching
of endless snacks (remember when we were
> two not three?) Now walking hand-
> in-hand is reserved for one large,
one grimy paw. And you're still
> looking for her to fix the. . .
for him to do the. . .
Purple no longer majestic but
> the mixture of primaries still
> a serenade by the window that suggests

III. He

He. He hee-hees. He almost sees

it. He. He rufous-red. He shrugs
                    off the dead. He sits. Faces the wolf.

He backlashed by she. He passes
                    the past off. No repast.

He helluva weekend. He
                    relieved to bring the key.

He in his study. Office. Zendo.
                    He carries everyone's story. He

lunches and does not see.
                    He walled by his wall.
Not at all. Says he. Re-
                    vered by patients, readers, meditators.

He leaves his crown when he
                    goes home. He
pours a drink.
                    By son dethroned.
He. Sleep alone.
                    He. Sometime wonder
where is she.

IV. She

Not tied by blood.
Not tied by time.
        Half a day painted over
        with fidgets, chores, blame.
The pigment-of-white thickens:
Oh if only she had a little poodle,
        a little noodle, a little. . .
        Airplanes are for thinking
of other getaways. Where's
the coupling in coupling?
        The bedsheets are creased
        paper with very little writing
on them. Except for the restless
boy who nightwalks to find her.
        And the smudged kiss—
does she even miss?

Sisypha Retires

Not pushing a rock—
like my husband, of erstwhile fame, Sisyphus,
I had been pulling him—a dead night-weight
on my chest—pulling the way sailors heave
up a three-thousand-pound mast so my fingers
had permanent rope-burn—pulling him to be
father, lover, other than self-
obsessed in his colossal task.
He would never rest. Always pushing
that stone, he became a stone. Sometimes
he called it the mind meditating; other times
he called it the weight of the world's tears
and he—only he—could blot them dry.
Little did I know he drank those tears—thrived on them.
So when I stopped crying, he stopped lifting me.

Then my work began of pulling—my son put to work—we both
began yanking—dragging—luring   his father away from that
anonymous ball of grief—my son pulling with chess pieces—
a baseball—his own monkey antics. I with lower-cut dresses. We yanked.
We tugged. We strained. We lugged till our hearts
beat into our lungs a Siren song. But we only saw
the back of his neck—the bristled head pushing out the door
pushing the air-like-granite pushing, finally, into another
woman—heaving her up the hill of his might
as we stayed below, encamped where his feet had been,
puling (puking into a pail) though by now his ears are stoppered.

So what could we do but let the line go—stop tugging at his back.
    Our arms and legs muscle-bound. Our faces, for once

        out of his shadow, have turned toward the unobstructed sun
and each other, the burden of his gravity lifted, we are beginning

to dance-as-though-swimming
                            to walk-as-though-floating.

Sunglasses in the Subway

I knew, was a very bad sign.
We'd just come from the marriage
counselor and what had he said?
What ice stormed my heart?
His declaring he'd lost all empathy
for me—his wife—this doctor
of empathy?
Or was it the argument over reading—
how I wanted him
to read with me in bed and
his refusal? So that now
on the subway, he announced
he would read. How is it
possible to use reading
as a weapon, a wounding shield?
The shutters slammed down
and there wasn't a peep-
hole of light   I sat
next to a Buddha of stone
and wept into the punishing fluorescence. Put
my dark glasses on to guard
me from the blinding shame and
the gaze of others.
But it failed me then
as our son's exuberant young
teacher—oblivious to pain—sitting
across the aisle with her husband
called out my name.

I had to come up from hell
and say hello (couldn't she tell?).
How was it possible? Not the reading, per se,
but the armoring as aggression.
As in the Mission chair
in his study into which he would retreat
each evening—the book
or newspaper more pressing than
his son or wife. The shutters
of his eyes slanted down onto
the lines of any novel. Once, when
I'd confronted him about lunch
with his lover he swore
was a friend, refusing
to cancel and have lunch with me,
that evening he scolded me
(why are the worst things
always true?)
for having moved a single book in the living room
and I raged at him in front
of our stunned son.
And what did he do?
He picked up the newspaper
and read as though untouched by
the whirlwind.
As though I had become Job
and he already my dead
husband.

Gnats

have infested the air the kitchen the living room even the bedroom   alighting
on my computer screen as I work or watch my arm   little killings I
perform against windows   daily smashing   sink—waiting food—page.
Where have they come from: the ficus plant—once a flood of golden blooms
it should have been a painting   dried and died and I clipped their umber heads
off   watered the stems until I couldn't stand it—stunted green things breeding
them—or was it the soil? Fetid. Something is rotten in the state of my life. Some
discord. Decay. Disused half of the bed. Invisible wound drawing out flies from
the aether   feeding off something—what?—my shrapneled heart? my slain
life as wife?—that has festered.

I keep killing them mid-flight
with a clap as they
slow—drunk

—some of them quite large with red eyes resting on walls just out of reach,
teeming at split tips of bruised bananas. I hate the way they're drawn to
the sink to drink—drown in my fear before I've drunk my tea—float
in my son's soup so nothing can be free of them. Flying at my face.
Making me face it. And face it. Left to rankle at having been defaced.
Replaced. Erased.

The Shame of the Adulterer's Wife

I.
Why is it I feel shame for his having left?
  In biblical times wouldn't the seducer
    have been stoned to death? Yet why do I
want to cover my face, the face of my poems
  where I proclaimed myself his "current wife"
    now fast becoming his "former wife"
far different from his "late wife"
  whose photo and urn he has taken with him, having already
    set them up once more —I am sure—as an everlasting shrine
to The Good Dead Wife?
  No. I am just the last in a receding procession of Deceived Women.
    Rancorous Women. Ungrateful Women.
Stringy-haired bitches who would grab
  any large kitchen knife and gut him like a ravening shark.
    Not ashamed to say it. Then of what? Of being The Scorned One?
The Spurned Woman? Wife? Mother and son as detritus?
  The cast aside? The obliterated? The erased? Lilith?

II.
    My gift to him for his fiftieth—
a dimpled d'Anjou pear
  monumental in its Gothic frame—
    left behind. Last summer's
last desperate offering—chocolate hearts wrapped in gold foil—
  left in the cheese drawer to grow colder each day.
    How can I eat them?
How can I not throw them away?

III.

Now that I shimmy
     shake every limb and ligament—rising and singing:
          lonely, lonely but sadly joyous each morning with the dog
lapping my face, my son—an abandoned Telemachus—
     roosting on the couch. Now, when I sew, I don't take
          my stitching out. Am beginning to conjure
suitors with my new necklaces and neckline. Am I
     ashamed of having groveled in vain for his heart's return?
          Ashamed at my own rejoicing I am free of him? Ashamed
I had sung his praises even after realizing I had been
     betrayed? A shame, isn't it, to waste more thought and time
          on what's beyond repair. Why wear the letter "A" (it's pinned on him)?
Why not choose "S" for the Sage
     I'm burning in this white room of the page to clear
          out—to smudge with smoldering his name (For shame!)
and any stock epithets upon me that remain.

Smudging: A Recipe

1. Imagine your body during sex after years of no sex or dancing after years of still hips. Like a hypnotic, you know what you are doing without knowing what you are doing.

2. Fill the metal pot to the brim with white sage—whole leaves and twigs.

3. Set it on the floor in the center of the empty room (the room that had harbored only books, a husk of a man) and

4. with a lit match start the burn to pungent smoke.

5. Close the door. Keep the dog out. Keep yourself out until it is done, until the smoke has consumed the room—all deceptions, remnants of a soul's shell that clenched and cleaved away inside its brittle cage.

6. Open the doors and windows. Let the air clear before you begin circling the room intoning, *Sh'ma Israel, Adonai Eloheinu, Adonai Echad. Sh'ma Israel. . .* over and over so the walls echo your calling down the Divine Presence filling the desert space with glory with praise with oneness with ecstatic coupling from your new-budding heart.

7. Next day hang up a clay plaque incised with the Ten Commandments in Hebrew so all Thou Shalts, Thou Shalt Nots will teem like no-see-ums like fireflies like bidden angels on the skin inside the soul the heart the breath of whoever now enters.

Ode to My Vajayjay

Vagina: "*Sheath* or *scabbard*"
First recorded usage in English:
Gibson's *Anatomy* (1682)

O *Vajayjay,* you sound far better than *vagina*—
        or *cut* or *slit* (as though someone
had to open you up
        as though you had not entranced
        since there *was* existence—
the embryo developing its primal folds).
Cunt: oldest of your names, in Old Norse:

Kunta, you include my button of fire my clit my inner
        lips—you're the one I like to say:
Fuck my cunt. Even writing it
        makes my vajayjay quiver.
All my Delight is a cunny in the Night: Cunny—
        close to cony or bunny, it's almost funny.
But *va-jay-jay* from *Gray's Anatomy* and Oprah
on TV is a-ok-ay with me.

O *jay-jay,* my pet birdie whose feathers will shutter away-ay
        if your hot beak gets stroked. You spasmed
until my son slithered out. O, the doctor cut you
        then he stitched you up—O pain O bleeding rain.
Now that the cramps, the dark blood of you is through—
        you're drier, not like my twenties
when you were a stream who sought
any vessel barge sub to float into—torpedo—you.

Yet still you linger, hunger for some dick.
   But holy is this hole
and what surrounds it.
                         In some African lands, even aborigines in Australia,
      they stitch you closed with needles or acacia thorns
and the husband has to burst you open like a bodice.
      How could they slice off your beating outer heart—source
of all your vibratos! You're the oldest instrument:
a plucked string in a chamber music solo

or else a duo or trio even a quartet (I haven't
      tried that yet). Prefer a single player
to layer my vajayjay with. A cunning
      cunnilinguist whose tongue's a moist pick
      with a moist prick. But even solo
                  since before I knew a name for you
I rubbed you up against running water
or a soft cloth. O Eve—when did you discover

it—"v" at the center of your name and being—
      our letter (*vulva* meaning "wrapper" or "uterus"—
oh, the male doctors still don't know what to make of us).
      Was the fruit you tasted first—alone—
your very own?

I Dreamed We Were

in
India,
he took
our son
to the Taj Mahal—
sinuous Moslem curves of
this mausoleum for a man's dead
wife—its monumental dome. When he
came back he gave me his back his razored
head. Why hadn't he taken me? My one sandal
missing. I hobbled to find it. Always the shrine to
the dead wife in our home. In her photograph she is
holding her elbows poised in life as in death. Never
a picture of me or our son. Now I'm one more angry
wife he's discarded. But I won't die. Won't commit
purdah. When I moved in I made one demand:

for her photograph	to be removed from
what was now our	bedroom. And his
response? You	shouldn't have
asked. I'll do	it. But you
should not	have asked.

Rags Meant

(pace T. S. E. & E. P.)

              which fragments can I shelve—
shore against my ruin

                 which shore can I ruin
myself against

               can I—against fragments—
soar

               can I fragment my ruin—
shelve my sore

                   shore my ire
(*"Slut!" "Bitch!"*)

               which ruined palm can I
sheer against (Ruse and)

            which palm against my fragments
rue

          alas, can I, against palms, be shorn—
(Erato)

             which keys against palms—
(my rune, my lyre)

            which fragment-key against

(my ruin, my liar)
can these keys—hostaged—palm

                    "slanging each other"
(fragments, shelved)

          my eye (hostaged heart) roam which
firmaments

        can I shore my ruined heart (shelved self)
fanging against the missing which

                 (*sous les palmiers*)

           can missing be shorn/shelled
(aghast my heart, liar his art)

          by which witch, a gent's, my palm—
halved

           ruined heart; shelved figment
(*sotto le rose)* can I hostage from

                which shore-misted I
ruined lair

          can art shore up shelved kisses (her)
(despair a part)

              unkeyed, unwe'd, unpalmed

—which ruined shore is this

II. Playing my Part

What I Knew

He figured I knew.
It suited him to figure I knew.
But I didn't know. Or I didn't know I knew.

When I asked him a leading question.
Until he alluded to it. When he could not really deny it.
As though we were both in on it.

As though the conversation had been ongoing
and not new.
He wanted me to know yet hid it.

He assumed I did know because he wanted it and he didn't want it.
Because he wanted not to have to say it. Not to have to face
the part of him that knew I didn't know. That knew I couldn't have known.

Or couldn't have known I knew and continued.

I didn't know I didn't want to know until I knew.
When I first knew I wanted to know more.
That was one of the many things he refused to let me know.

Now that I already knew. Now that I already knew that I knew.
These being the things I will never know.
Because in the end he didn't want me to know.

He didn't want part of himself to know.

For the Alabaster Figure from the Cyclades

Something   in her pose
her arms crossed over
        or slightly beneath
                her breasts   is she holding herself
                together from some great blow?
        Or merely standing self-possessed?
Or is she ashamed to be so
        exposed to the centuries'
                raw gaze? She crouches
                yet stands on her toes—
        a stance it's hard to imagine
a real woman maintaining
        her balance   her head—
                a flattened-out mask
                no mouth only
        a nose carved out so
the eye sockets are hinted
        at. As generic as they come.
                Or is she? I saw
                the genuine ones
        in Naxos—thousands of years
old—bought this reproduction
        in Athens in the Plaka
                the night before we flew home
                (there were hundreds like her).
        When my fate (I knew but didn't know)
was sealed.   Something
        impervious
                about her. Something solid

and enduring. She holds
herself despite everything
that has happened. As I would have to
hold myself through the long summer
and fall. I wanted her
in my life. Her singular pose.
(What color, what consistency the walls
of a fractured heart?)
The folds above her sex say the sculptor
understood she might have
given birth. I carried her
in my flight bag
sobbed in my seat
next to a self-clefted stone.
I sensed she would protect me.
That I would have to clasp
hold of myself. Her body
the color of this winter's absent
snow. Her bent knees enduring
some as yet unforeseen
burden. Her head lifted above
suffering. Or else calling
to her god, knowing that the
men of the earth
would not come to her aid, nor
redress her wrongs.

The Shell

I lived inside with him—
    at least I thought I did.
        Call it the nacre of marriage.
          I whirled inside
its whorls
    with my son. Chambers within
        chambers. I often lost
          sight of him—my husband.
Increasingly so. He moved
    to an outer chamber even
        as we limped along the beach
          his hands pocketed in their tombs—
was I inside or outside? For years
    it sat on my shelf—
        a mollusk with radiating
          points. I never thought
to pick it up. Examine too closely
    whether the creature still lay
        within. Until now,
          or back then, last summer
when I asked him where he'd been
    and he refused to answer. I turned
        the shell over—the one I'd
          been living in and it was
empty. Why did I still
    want to live within
        its ghostly chambers?
          Why do I still live

within them? Now my heart
        echoes with the no
                footfalls of him.
                        I am in a darker vault
scratching to get out.
        Winding through
                so many rooms—
                        the dead-end corridors of years
of his being body-shed.
        Why did it take so long to see
                he'd vanished—a hermit crab gone
                        to a new-old shell to armor
himself within.
        I'm staying inside
                this old whelk.
                        Unwelcomed.
Put the shell of self up to
        my ear. The rushing
                sound of his tide tearing
                        himself away.
My whooshing heart. My hard
        to follow. Hard to hold
                on. The whorls
                        flattened out into a tunnel
I know I must crawl
        through—on all fours
                with the boy
                        on my back and a steady
lapping if not of waves then of
        a wheezy dog
                at my face.

Eurydice's Testimony

It's true he came down
to bring me back.
When he spied me—dugs
hollowed out, skin no longer

cover to bone, hair
almost gone—
he turned
(not back

to look at me)
for some other
woman he could call
wife.

When I tripped
and fell
into the netherworld
he let me go

when it was too late
he turned back
into the singing snake
he had once charmed

and been.
So I slid further back
refused his gaze,
which would have killed me

twice.

The Necklace

The emerald's "grass-lamp glow" is better.
—Marianne Moore

I, too, disliked it. No—even hated it. Not poetry, but the diamond
hard eye of him to engage
me. Can a marriage last
when it is founded on a mis-
understanding?
I said I hated

diamonds; he heard I hated rings. He rung me wrong. So, what he gave and I wore
for thirteen years was a diamond
necklace—eye of missed-the-
point—my flashing hair shirt. Its point
pierced—dug in—to
my skin. It wore me

as the sign—daily—nightly—of having given in. When what I'd wanted
was an emerald. Sapphire. Any-
thing but the blistering bright
of a sliver of night. Compressed
coal of Super-
man. Of forever

meaning never. When the pledge was broken by the diamond saw of his heart
I nearly flung it in Great Pond
the way he'd flung his dead
wife's ashes years before—not tell-
ing me until
after I had been

swimming among them. I vowed instead to keep it. Never wear it again. That
stinging nettle of not-right light.
Thrust in a drawer of flawed
things: the gold band engraved *My Be-*
loved is mine soon
to follow. Unlike

the emerald: *what keeps life from becoming a parcel of uniformities.*
Why not wear a Nile-green string
of spun glass. Peridot
ring (facsimile from one in
a Van Dyke por-
trait)—if not emerald,

then sea-green spirals of Venetian glass at my wrist. Write this with a jade-green
Sheaffer Lifetime Fountain Pen
from the 1930s
with (what else?) green ink from *Campo*
Marzio Roma.
How a husband could

get me so wrong. Then wrong me
further. Not keep
me. Never really

get me at all.

Playing My Part

I let him go. I complied. Adjusted. Saw. Did not see his disappearing
    act of staying while leaving the body. It felt so familiar.
        My zombie-mom (on Stelazine, Thorazine to tamp

        her paranoia down), would be there/not there to make
    macaroni-and-cheese, do the wash, help me with my Spanish.
I knew she was sick, I knew she loved me though she lay in bed until noon,

again in the afternoon, comatose with the *New York Post*, her arm bent
    at the elbow to cover her face. This was what love could feel like—
        somnolent, absent. Why be paranoid when he slept in the same pose.

        Sometimes cooked dinner, did the wash. Who knew a blunt face
    could hold so much hate. The child in me saw his numbing out,
going to bed early, not as aversion but a version of my mother's love

and all I had to do—as when she'd be taken away, hospitalized, shocked—
    was wait for his return. (Is there a Penelope inside every troubled wife?)
    Didn't my mom always come back?

Gaslit

Or call it byte-lit. Instead of crawling around
    the attic like Charles Boyer and making the gaslights dim
    he scrawled e-mails—love notes—he said were not there

so that words assumed a pallor, a white-on-white like our son's
    invisible ink, his affection vanishing beneath the mouthed screen
    of *I love you*. How the wish to believe makes it all mirror-writing:

what I wanted was what I got. How she must have stood with him
    on the other side of their one-way mirror, laughing. How I peered
    in to see my own troubled gaze. And then anger. How angry,

ungrateful, he showed me I'd become. At which I grew angrier.
    How lying relies on receding mirrors of lying so that the self
    is never caught. At least now I can retreat and roll the movie

I didn't know I was in—the one he repeats with every woman (those angry
    ungrateful women)—so that events screen themselves: like the time
    we stood on the subway platform and I popped some gum in my mouth

and he ranted, accused me of ruining the evening. That the movement of my jaws
    (which I had to know he hated) ruined the foreplay in bed. That he wanted it
    ruined so he could sleep in the other room alone with her

e-mails. That the one turning up the gas in the attic breathes in those self-fumes.
    Gaslit: the only way to explain his asking my permission to see her
    for dinner when he was already trysting her at lunch. Relieved, I breathed

those sweet fumes up, not wanting to see what I didn't want to see:
the only night he ever came home late was after that dinner,
when I pretended to be asleep. Which I was.

To a Jumbo Sea Worm at the Aquarium in Cornwall

Aquarium staff have unearthed a "giant sea" worm that was attacking coral reef and prize fish. The 4ft long monster, named Barry, had launched a sustained attack on the reef in a display tank.

—*Daily Mail*

Devourer of bait traps—caught hiding, dining
on coral reef

what made you bite through a 20-pound fishing line
in the middle of the night?

Mysterious terrorizer of fish
with stinging bristles

that could numb someone for life,

killing and eating whole fish bodies,
even injuring a Blue Tang,

your looks alone half-paralyze—is that why
you only come out at night?

Dark greasy brown with fangs for maw,
hornlike antennae, and black holes for eyes,

who knew a worm could be the length of a sci-fi scream
(unmagnified)?

Poor giant sea worm. Now that they've caught you
on camera, named you Barry, their new pet-monster,

no longer a secret, have you lost your bite? Wasn't
your predator's bliss being surreptitious?

Char'd Endings

a cento

Of ruined and transcendent lovers
There is no absence that cannot be replaced
In their carnivorous landscape
It's you my father who are changing
Leaning on your reflection in the window
Already the oil rises from the lead again
Beloved! Feel the dark planting waken
Woman breathes, Man stands upright
The earth loved us a little I remember
Like a horse aimless at his bitter plowing
Failure is of no moment, even if all is lost
Everything swoons into transiency
Keep us violent and friends to the bees on the horizon
Such is the heart
I hurt and am weightless

To My Orange Reading Glasses

When I unclasp   your tangerine arms
from my temples   the close-up of you

goes blurry—Window dresser. Menu   diviner.   Without you
the *New York Times* becomes   a snail's trail.

I can   no longer read the strength
inside your arm without   you on.   And then, how can I?

Ghost's   glasses. Windshield   wipers.
My driving along the page is ruled by you.   Or else

I'm a drunken   swerver who can't read
the signs. If I had worn you   more   would I have seen the purloined lies

before they came up through the floor?   Seen the pocketed hands
like silenced puppets   for what   would not be said?

Divined the space between   frames   fraught with absence?
Oh parser of prayer   now you're cracked along

your left brim   as if to say: *All things crack and
break down eventually, don't*   *they?*

Not a Vase

after Giorgio Morandi

Not clay   pitcher   oil can   not
rectangular   solid coalescing
                           into
tableware
not fore/
aft of perspec-
tive not
terracotta   earthenware not   glass   porcelain not
marble not   stone
                            or bone not

useful or open to   predilections   of decay or form

red chalk: what blood   sour-dries to
                                   Grizzano
inscape of
dull ochre & sandstone   not
lined up
to be domino'd   not perfect cylinders
of rough order not
bud vases
milk pitchers
amphoras   not urns   from Greek hearths or ships' holds
each one an instance of
not again
again
knot of not
not nugatory

not clay pitcher   fruit bowl   not oil can
small nugget of having looked
at the overlooked
          not terracotta   earthenware not   porcelain

nulled annulled   so that curves of
          have the force of

not marble   not stone   not nullipara
     having birthed your quizzical gaze

not annealed but softening not glazed over
          not vases

so that to see   has become   a discipline
          a turning away
     from turning away

Knot His to S[t]ay

as that first New Year's thirteen years ago
        Palm Springs [pals ring] / as cold to

                                as sails fold in the seen breeze

as turquoise patches as the sea

                                now how to rid myself of his expressions:

go and cool off your hot head

                                as now tearing up when I do

all the phrases that limn a together

                                as called me *Girlfriend* [*current*]

Oh replaceable me . . .   *It's only a matter of time*
{as called him *boy*—

                                by his dad}

as call me *plaintiff* (placemark) on the grounds of
        [as were prior wives]

                                cruel and unusual treatment
what does it mean to be true, your Honour?

                                adultery

as words housing a heart?
what does it mean usual treatment?   (acted out in a hotel or her office)

as what he showed me:

                        the breeze blowing through

(no words left)

                        his ribcage   bone-heart

[*sleeping with her?*]

how a question becomes a trial: [*are you . . .*]

[*fucking her?*]

I don't want to answer that

[*on the grounds that may . . .*

unground me]

as though the answer [*are you?*] had to be

ferreted out of [unutterable]

as though a pattern exists

a paisley turpitude
[in blacks and greys]

of court proceedings
in place of self-righteous stripes

that pinned him

evidence: he clipped his fingernails

[one of the last acts]

in flagrante   on the street corner

carefully, meticulously

across from

Wellfleet Town Hall

here I rest my case

as wouldn't be needing them anymore

as [forcibly] got himself driven off
to his new lover

by my friend

[*delicto*]

my honor? how could I have

                                        traded everything [the *very* thing] for

[a stable table / shifting tectonic plates]
lost even that?

                                        his arms his [em/pathetic]

eyes emptied   brittle caged [un/excavated] heart   that broke

at the first cry of
                  our son   as fountain hymn I [hummed]

as with two spigots for *him*   [not for him]

Should Have

Checked the sign.   Held onto the string.
Learned to cook.   Returned the book.   His look.
His graze of my back.   Been less
sexed at thirty.   Humbler at forty.
More inscrutable at fifty.   Seen in the dark.
Averted my eyes from the sun.   Fired her.
Said yes to the toke.   Locked out the black dog.
Gotten off at the last stop.   Never looked
back.   Stayed in Bologna.   Heard the whispered word.
Jumped from the moving car.   Dived
in.   Refused
to be shamed.   Said no
to every couple.   Learned Mandarin.
Gone home alone.
                    Flown to her deathbed.
Drunk at his Bris.   Called her back from
the platform.   Spent more
on less.   Told every secret.
Admired more lines.   Returned every kiss
or hiss.   Played the violin.   Let him go.
Moved to.   Stayed put.   Never
looked back.   Slammed him harder.
Dug my own pond.   Planted a garden.   Learned to swim sooner.
     Kept going in
Had another child.   Weaned this one
sooner.   Stayed happy with
Forgiven more quickly.   Laughed from the belly.   Sang more.
Never compared myself with others.   Never been late.
Never said never.   Never.   Looked.   Back.

Desire and the Lack

When I lacked
desire my love unlatched

his key from me and soon
I lacked a lackey. Deserted,

unstirred, to no sir inured.
Once lacking , desire grew

for a sire. Now
desire what I lack

am nearly lack-

luster, abandoned,
conspire with abandon

for the bandoneon
player—layer-on of love

and blandishments.
There is an ache in lack

when I wake on my back
oh what I lack: a sharp *ach!*

What song more plaintive
than the lone key of me?

The moan key of monkey
me to let go desire? What

ire is higher
than to find a liar where

I had once been desired.
(now deserted, de-sired)

my unplucked heart
lyre in the dawn wind

ready to be strummed
into fire.

III. Happiness Is Luck

I was in a whirlwind, now I'm in some better place.
—Bob Dylan

Phonography

The first time, early morning, he asked to hear—no, to see, really—how
    the phonograph worked:
how the arm with the needle moved across the turntable then down
    onto the huge spinning licorice disk.
I pulled out the three-album recording from Woodstock, slid out the middle record,
    then put down the side where Jefferson Airplane sang,
always half-intelligibly to me, to look what's going on in the streets:
    Gotta revolution. Got to revolution.
With Grace Slick I did the monkey there in my bedroom at 8:30 in the morning
    in the early days of 2005
nearly thirty-six years later, as my six-year-old looked on. What could he understand
    from that time—too young to realize
we were there all over again: the young men, and women this time,
    dying in ambush in the desert—
instead of the jungle—the massacres, the tortures, and we still
    needing some music to magnify our passion?
Why does that moment with him looking on have a shimmer, even an aura
    around it, so years from now
as years from back then, when I was thirteen and just slightly too young
    to have been there, still I was there
even as I was caught in Brooklyn, not yet smoking pot?
    Why is that yearning still palpable—
that moment all these years later, whatever there was to remember I still remember:
    the deceit in high places, our need
for a revolution so that in twelve years my own son won't have to dodge the draft
    with his long hair and his wild ideas
he'll be sure I can't conceive of, but will contain echoes of something
    I have nearly lived.

Forward Sestina (Dylanesque)

I
Want
You
So
Bad
Honey

Honey
I'm
Bad to
Want
So much of
You

You are not my
Honey
So what can
I do but
Want to be
Bad

Bad I am with or without
You who
Wants only
Honey and that's what
I am   would give you
So   so   so tongue-tied am I

So lip-stitched so
Bad at say-signaling
I would do for   to   with
You who are nothing but
Honey, and how I
Want to oh how I

Want
So . . .
(Honey, Coney)
Bad
You and
I

For I Will Consider the Overlooked Dragonfly

How it is often a damselfly, skimmer, or darner
How it belies the idea that we invented neon
How it mates while in flight, laying eggs on the pond's lilies
How its blues are purples, its browns, reds
How unfearful it is of the human body
How one will come to bask on my forearm, foot, or the arm of my deck chair
How I praise the way it eats the larvae of biting insects
How a Variable Dancer in lavender and black alighted as I wrote this
For I praise them, not needing to search for dragonflies (the way birders search for
    birds) but let them fly to me
For sometimes their wings have stigma and in the wind I watch their wings and
    abdomen sway while their head and thorax are still
For this one's a male whose spider-web wings and abdomen are tipped sky-blue
For might it be the same damselfly that alights on the arm of my chair as I write
For his bulgy compound eyes, what do they see
For his violet thorax the color of a flower
For the honeybees grazing the sea honeysuckle
    and the hummingbirds on the mimosa blooms
For their pond world which is oblivious to names
For ours with its naming obsession
For the only way I desire to catch one is with the net of my eyes
For some say a damselfly is a weak flier compared to a dragonfly
For the male clasps the female's head with the end of its abdomen when mating
For we call mating pairs a copulation wheel but I say they look like a backwards 3
For it flies from spring through late summer (though they live for only a few weeks)
For some darters and skimmers migrate south and the ones returning are their
    children or grand- or great-grandchildren or

For after the storm a male white-faced Meadowhawk, its thorax and abdomen
    pomegranate-red, has come to bask in the windy sun
For the wind, the wind, which causes a stirring within the stillness
    and a stillness within the stirring

With You

There's so much that I want to do with you.
My mind already feels like it's been glued with you.

Wandering the blue-jay way
My body wants to be in tune with you.

Meditating, reading *War and Peace* in bed,
I even feel I can be blue with you.

It's too early (second week) to share this song:
I'd like to come over and cook legumes with you.

Get a grip, girl, you'd say. *Don't pant and ache.*
All our hurts, I know I would undo with you.

I've only seen your face on-screen.
Is it too soon to say I'd never be untrue with you?

Your grizzled chin, your gravelly voice, your punning wit:
Can I help it if I'm the loving loon with you?

If these words could slow my heart,
When we meet, I'd try and be so cool with you.

You're Wood-Goat, I'm Fire-Monkey;
My nature's so impatient to spoon with you.

Foehn

(warm dry wind coming off the mountain)

Foehn that drifts from my mons
to you, my man. No one
has ever wafted that breeze
as you have done. Gone down
my hummock, my tussock
into what underground streams

fly-fished there for what has
spawned in the narrows
without hooks
bobbed & sunk thick fruit
to see what might pool
up from below unfathomed
unfathomable. How you
reach and keep finding me
beneath the hanging garden

formerly unvisited—
with its fountain of mud-
hued tadpoles and cir-
culating koi—now open
all hours to you
my gardener, keeper
of my vineyard whose
vintage is reserved for you
my olive run—first pressed
that oohs and oozes out
for the two of us.

As Ants, in Their Dark Company, Will Touch

so lustful souls embrace in friendship
so the blue damselfly alighting on my knee
so the darkening wheel of the moon

so the chipmunk's nervous chittering
approach and then scampering retreat . . .
Comparisons are endless but

to what purpose? If poetry is this world's
impulse to find resemblance in remembrance—
then what if you decide to open

the page as a breeze lifts
your hair, scatters too-ripe leaves, plops
a bullfrog with its one-note banjo twang

sets the cicada's electric buzz when the sun is hot:
all these movements toward expressions of the self
—yellow jacket's spittle-forming its grey-

paper nest in the playground where children,
ignorant of the risk of being stung, climb and swing.
What if nothing resembles anything else—what is beyond

like or *as*, beyond the embrace of thing for thing?
Paradise? The grave? Knots in the deck planks
are weathered eyes that don't see but mark a point

of focus (see you can't stop comparing). As children shouting
from the other shore—the longed-for place of memory—so the soul's
calling out before they can be allowed to cross out of the land

of this and that. And what are the darning needles marrying
each other mid-air in a double-decker waltz but a contraction
of words—what I mistakenly heard as *dining needles*

as a child? As if lovemaking were a feast.

From the Cricket Cage

Bamboo toothpicks for roof and walls, pegged in place for the house cricket.

The singing cricket chirps through the long night, wrote Bei Ju-Yi.

The only snow the steel cricket knows is dust.

What is born in summer? Dead by spring?

Always too large to flit through the door: Good-Luck cricket.

In fall, the ladies of the palace keep crickets in gold cages near their pillows
  to hear their night songs, wrote Tian Bo.

Antennae to Time: when the season changes the cricket is still . . .

In Shanghai's insect market, peddlers sell Jia Ge-Ge (singing brothers).

The boy wants to take the cricket out, perch it on his palm to watch it fly.

Only the male cricket sings, so she must be a Jie-Er (singing sister).

The mother was once the cricket-girl; her father built the cage around her.

To woo, to fight, to sound an alarm. On the front leg, right below the elbow,
  female cricket listens.

Inside the pages of her sleep, cricket.

Cricket-Emperor, so-called because he loved cricket fighting.

In early spring, when pear trees snow their infinite white petals, no cricket.

On the eleventh floor, in the corner of the smallest room, filled with mute bars
  of books, cricket.

Small yellow bell, inky bell, stony bell, bamboo bell, pagoda bell, painted mirror:
  names of fighting crickets.

Born as white nymphs, in one month crickets darken, begin to sing.

Inside her Tai Chi slipper, cricket.

On a summer's eve, or wet, in spring thicket, cricket.

There's a ricket in cricket. A crick in the neck of this line.

Red-winged blackbirds call.
Tall grasses. Pussy willows.
Summer shirr, crickets.
Silent in her cage for thirty-five years: heirloom cricket.
Let this be her song.

Inamorato: A Triolet

You're my oboe beaux, my oh-boy of woe
      Met by chance, now we compose a contredanse.
I'm your cello (duo, solo), please pluck me pizzicato,
My oboe beaux, my woe boy no mo.
Crescendo, diminuendo—all my strings—obbligato, vibrato.
      We met perchance, is this our contredanse?
My oh-boy of woe (no more), now my oboe beaux,
With one glance—mumchance—(no) dalliance in this romance.

If Happiness is Luck

the happenstance of you
the hap of us
now how get to the haptic
hush of us   the to-be-
touched   (so left to chance)
if lips will more than

if hips   to find bliss in the slipped
moment   how happed upon
we are   I say we when
you and me so shift-
ing are these I might get free

to bewilder in the wilderness of me

so remonstranced in romance
(do we bristle) how hap turns to hope-
less how to make a haply
out of this now and this
and this   I ope my heart
too readily   my haptic heart

my hope sometime betimes mishap
Oh am I become Mis(s)Hap   are you the to-be-
missed happening   my backward glance   my sigh
within why (not)
to be a we   to happen in this instance
upon our stance   (our happenstance)   happily

Now that

Now that my bleeding moons are gone
      Now that his seed is spent   Now that

my heart is a dashed
      pomegranate and his blood knifes

his days with night   Now that
      I am pregnant only with words

and he has wrapped himself
      in a shield of notes

Now that my ribcage is a ruined tower
      and his neck a hive

of stinging flies
      Now that loss is my glittering

possession
      and without

the raspy air he coughs
      Now that

my body of sighs
      is his thumbprint

and his palm stroke
      the backwards clock I shutter by

Duende

Why disturb the abrupt gone of you as if I could
conjure you out of words, out of my stunned life—

out of yours? Why unearth one more *if only* (that week
we saw flamenco—a man with duende, his body bitten by Death,

rapping it out on the wooden floor—three nights later, your Death-
thrall over your staccato'd heart, to become the flailing   blood-

fist in the punched-out wall   broken-up chairs   inside   before
your naked fall outside the running shower into frozen)?

Didn't you know what you risked for your duende? Didn't I know
what I risked fleeing mine? Why fling myself upon the air

for more than a decade, only your bones and beard
underground in a hut cut off from light? Am I still trying

to fathom your duende? Or my own? Now that I'm thawing,
isn't it still from your death I have to step? To castanet?

Gypsy Ballad

after Lorca

Blue how you'll ride me blue.
Blue hair. Blue mouth.
Hips on the bed,
crickets on the screen.
With chest of night,
he sleeps on his arm,
blue belly, flanks dark blue,
and his eyes, mud-gold.
Blue how you'll ride me blue.
Beneath the sweating cloud,
someone is calling to him
but he can't hear.

Blue how I'll ride you blue.
Small beads of rain
fly up with the fireflies—
the eyes of midnight are opening.
The almond tree sways in
the blue wind with its
blue-lobed fruit, and the cactus,
guardian of his blue pain,
prickles his skin in the damp wind.
But how will he come? From which
direction following which blue map?
Still he rests his head on his hand,
his blue belly, flanks dark blue.
Hips on the bed.

Notes

The book epigraph is from Franz Kafka's *The Zürau Aphorisms,* trans. by Michael Hofmann, intro. by Roberto Calasso (Schocken Books, 2006).

"Ode to Nitrous Oxide": the epigraph is from Edward Rothstein, "A Mind-Altering Drug Altered a Culture as Well," *The New York Times,* May 5, 2008.

"Unpairing: Proofreading My Marriage": "ketuba" is the Jewish marriage contract; "get" is the religious divorce document.

"First Words, Last Words": the epigraph is from Raymond P. Scheindlin's translation of *The Book of Job* (Norton, 1998), 6:26, p. 67.

"The Necklace": the epigraph is from Marianne Moore's poem "Voracities and Verities Sometimes Are Interacting" and "what keeps life . . ." is from "Emeralds," *The Poems of Marianne Moore,* ed. Grace Schulman (Viking, 2003), pp. 272 and 35.

"To a Jumbo Sea Worm at the Aquarium in Cornwall": the epigraph is from "Barry the giant sea worm discovered by aquarium staff after mysterious attacks on coral reef," *The Daily Mail Online,* March 31, 2009.

"Char'd Endings": a cento composed of the last lines of poems by René Char, *Selected Poems,* trans. by Mary Ann Caws and Tina Jolas (New Directions, 1992).

Happiness Is Luck: the epigraph is from Bob Dylan's song "Something There Is About You," Copyright © 1973 by Ram's Horn Music; renewed 2001 by Ram's Horn Music.

"Phonography": the line is from Jefferson Airplane's "Volunteers," by Paul Kantner and Marty Bailin. Copyright © BMI, 1969.

"If Happiness Is Luck" is indebted to Lyn Hejinian's *Happily* (Post Apollo Press, 2000).

"As Ants, in Their Dark Company, Will Touch": the title is from Dante's *Purgatorio* (XXVI. 34-35), trans. Allen Mandelbaum (Bantam, 2004).

"Duende" is for Billy, in memory, always.

Acknowledgements

With gratitude to the following publications where these poems first appeared, some in earlier versions:

Alaska Quarterly Review: "For I Will Consider the Overlooked
    Dragonfly"
Antioch Review: "The Shell"
Best American Poetry Blog (online): "Gypsy Ballad"
Barrow Street: "Unpairing: Proofreading My Marriage"
The Cortland Review (online): "Sunglasses in the Subway"
Court Green: "From the Cricket Cage"
Drunken Boat (online): "The Shame of the Adulterer's Wife"
Ducts (online): "Scenes From an Ideal Marriage"
5 a.m.: "To the Furies Who Visited Me in the Basement of Duane Reade"
580 Split: "Rags Meant"
Guernica: A Magazine of Art & Politics (online): "Ode to Nitrous Oxide"
Iowa Review: "Inamorato: A Triolet," "With You"
MARGIE: "After My Husband Moved Out His Things"
New American Writing: "Desire and the Lack"
New Republic: "Sisypha Retires"
NOR (New Ohio Review): "Playing My Part"
Parthenon West: "Char'd Endings"
Ploughshares: "The Tip"
Poetry International: "Duende"
Pool: "Should Have"
Prairie Schooner: "Phonography," "Forward Sestina (Dylanesque)"
RUNES: "As Ants, in Their Dark Company, Will Touch"
Southampton Review: "The Necklace," "For the Alabaster Figure From
    the Cyclades," "Foehn"

Spillway: "I Dreamed We Were"
Washington Square Review: "Not A Vase"

"To the Furies Who Visited Me in the Basement of Duane Reade" was awarded The Pushcart Prize and published in *Pushcart Prize: Best of the Small Presses,* vol. 35, ed. Bill Henderson (Pushcart Press, 2011).

"For the Alabaster Figure From the Cyclades" was reprinted in *Phati'tude: A Literary Magazine,* in the issue "Ekphrasis: A Conversation Between Poets & Artists."

"Char'd Endings" was reprinted in *The Cento: A Collection of Collage Poems* (Red Hen Press, 2011).

"For I Will Consider the Overlooked Dragonfly" was reprinted in *Ecopoetry: A Contemporary American Anthology,* ed. Ann Fisher Wirth and Laura-Gray Street (Trinity University Press, 2012).

"Inamorato: A Triolet" was reprinted in *Discoveries: New Writing from The Iowa Review* (The University of Iowa Press, 2012).

I want to thank all of my friends and fellow poets who have believed in me and helped me through the whirlwind. Special thanks to Jeff Friedman, Phillis Levin, Ellen Geist, Ann Fisher-Wirth, Evan Eisenberg, and Ruby Namdar for their astute suggestions. I owe a depth of gratitude to Ed Ochester for being a judicious editor and for giving a home to this book. Finally, I want to express my appreciation to The Corporation of Yaddo, The MacDowell Colony, and Fundación Valparaiso, where some of these poems were written or revised.